THE LIVING ALPHABET

ABCDEFG
HIKLMNO
PQRSTVXY

WARREN CHAPPELL

THE LIVING ALPHABET

The University Press of Virginia
Charlottesville

THE UNIVERSITY PRESS OF VIRGINIA
Copyright © 1975 by the Rector and Visitors
of the University of Virginia

First paperback printing 1980

Library of Congress Cataloging in Publication Data
Chappell, Warren, 1904–
    The living alphabet.

    1. Alphabet. I. Title.   P211.C47   471'.1   75-5884
ISBN 0-8139-0873-6

Printed in the United States of America

CONTENTS

I · BACKGROUND
1

II · ANATOMY
13

III · ROMAN CAPITALS
23

IV · ROMAN SMALL LETTERS
35

V · THE LIVING ALPHABET
41

Afterword
49

THE LIVING ALPHABET

I BACKGROUND

THE ROMAN ALPHABET must be the most universal tool that Western man has created by and for his intellect, but it should be added that his understanding and care of it are hardly more developed than for his commonest implements of the field. It is not necessary to be able to write beautifully in order to appreciate beautiful writing, although it is imperative that in making aesthetic judgments, knowledge must share a place with instinct. It is the *spirit* of letterforms that is important, and just as the human spirit is elusive and indefinable, so is the spirit of carved, written, and printed words.

It seems natural to refer to the *spirit* and the *letter* in the case of laws. It should be no less natural to speak of *spirit* and *law* with reference to letters. Webster defines *spirit* as "the animating or vital principle giving life to phys-ical organisms." And the centuries have provided no end of *laws*, that is, of rules and guides for designing and rendering the twenty-six letters in all their ameliorations. However, there remains some essence that defies capture and organized descriptions, yet is a recognizable, common denominator in all great inscriptions, manuscripts, and typefaces. It is the manifestation that can be said to give the work its "breath of life," another of Webster's definitions of *spirit*.

John Howard Benson points out that Euclid's word στοιχειον, which is translated as *element*, is the same as the common Greek word for *letter*. Thus geometric elements and letters have a common identification. It may be helpful to point out, in the beginning, that the alphabet is a series of improvisations on geometric elements, and it is fair to say that any-

1

one who can understand the forms of Roman capitals, as they were executed in the early centuries of the Christian era, and who can recreate them in composition with distinction, is certain to have the basis for appreciating all the variations made in those archetypes during the succeeding eighteen centuries.

Edward Johnston has written that "developing or redeveloping an art involves the tracing in one's own experience of a process resembling its past development." His statement is essentially a basic law of biology that says: *ontogeny recapitulates phylogeny*, or, the development of an individual organism recapitulates the development of a kind or type of animal or plant. However, the natural law that mandates tadpolehood for every frog does not necessarily contain the magic that can make a prince of him. Nor is long apprenticeship a substitute for genius in design. As Whistler said, "anyone can learn to draw, but God Almighty alone can make him an artist."

Paleography, the study of ancient writing, is both fascinating and rewarding, but such study is not really necessary in order to set the stage for the Roman alphabet. To understand its development, it is enough to know that this alphabet was derived from the Greeks, who in turn borrowed from the Phoenicians. Letters from the Greek and Phoenician (Semitic) alphabets are closely related in names, forms, and order. For example, *alpha* and *beta*, the names of the first and second letters of the Greek alphabet, are derived from the Semitic *aleph* and *beth*.

The letterforms we use stem from *lapidary Roman capitals*, incised with a chisel, that came to full flower in the early Christian era. The classic model is the inscription on the column erected in Rome about A.D. 114 by the Emperor Trajan (frontispiece). The Latin alphabet consisted of twenty letters of Greek origin, plus G, Y, and Z. The letters U, W, and J, added centuries after the Trajan inscription, brought the total number up to our present twenty-six characters. U and W are outgrowths of the V form. The letter J, which appeared last, is an alternate form of I.

The symbols that compose our alphabet are phonograms; they are phonetic rather than pictorial; they stand for sounds rather than objects. They have, in fact, reached an advanced stage of simplification, where they represent elementary sounds in a progressive change from signs as syllables, and previously signs as words. Before phonograms, there were ideograms, a more primitive alphabet in which symbols stood for either objects or concepts.

By the ninth century B.C., the Greeks had learned to write. At first, they wrote lines from right to left; for a time they alternated lines right to left, then left to right. Finally, the line was carried from left to right, as it is today.

Latin manuscripts go back to the first century A.D., and it is important to note that the physical act of writing plays an ever-increasing part in the development of letterforms. Also, the tools used to produce letters have always been formative forces in evolving their character, shape, and rhythm.

The great monumental Roman letters may be thought of as having simple geometric bones, so fleshed-out that the straights and curves relate organically. A letter should seem to be of one piece, not a sum of its parts. The round forms are circles and parts of circles. Notable efforts have been made to develop formulae for the construction of the alphabet. Those made by Luca Pacioli, Albrecht Dürer, and Geofroy Tory are certainly among the most successful. But no set of rules can be slavishly held to. The subtleties of the great Roman forms have always eluded the compass and the square. The perfect expression of a

3

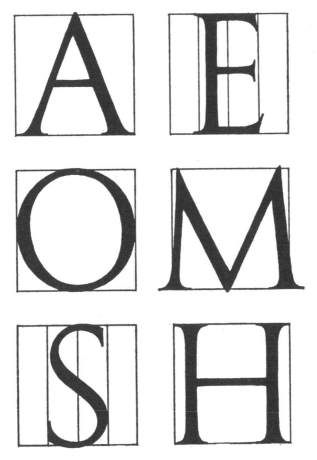

letter remains in the mind of the artist, as a pure concept of form. Just as a draughtsman uses a model for a figure drawing, a letter artist must use memory of the ideal form, along with the lettering tool in his hand, to respond to the special requirements of his design.

There are several ways of reaching a general understanding of the basic nature of Roman. One logical way is to think of the forms as a series of geometrical variations on a theme of square, circle, and triangle, which, when set together, will become a frieze of contracting and expanding spatial interruptions. This breathing quality is the essence of the inscriptional concept and is responsible for the liveliness as well as the nobility of the great classic letter carvings. Almost every letter has its contained space, that in type is called the *counter* and is related, in type composition, to the separations between letters. This inner, contained space is not only vital to the color of a letterform—its black-and-white value—but is an integral part of it as well.

If, in visualizing Roman, one thinks of the shapes in relationship to square fields, proportions can be more dramatically understood structurally, and the variations from narrow E to wide M become clearer as skeletal archetypes. Here, several letters based on the Trajan capitals are set against a square field.

The thick-and-thin characteristics of these examples indicate their development from written forms produced with a flat-edged tool. In Pompeii, which was destroyed in the first century A.D., there remain examples of mural writing made with a flat brush. This was an obvious way to lay in an inscription that was to be incised in stone. And thus the antiquity of the flat-edged instrument, in shaping the appearance of Western alphabets, is established. The centuries between Emperor Trajan and Printer Gutenberg were to be dominated

LITTERA SCRIPTA MANET

by calligraphy that was written with reeds and with quills sharpened to a wedge-shaped point.

The more formal written alphabet of this early Roman period was known as *square capitals.*

These capitals were used for the writing of the more important works from the second to the fifth century. In their proportions, they had much in common with the lapidary capitals, differing chiefly in the strong contrasts of thick-and-thin and in the serifs derived from the use of the pen. A serif is a terminal device, functionally employed to strengthen lines which would otherwise fall away optically. This is especially true of incised lines. By using a chisel in such a way that the finishing cuts were widened, a stonecutter produced a strong bracketed terminal.

Square capitals are not easy to write, and

5

their wide usage was limited. The story of writing can be told in terms of the search for ever-simpler forms, requiring fewer strokes and fewer lifts of the pen. Simpler forms carried their own beat, or rhythm, to such an extent that spacing for color and legibility could be ever more easily controlled.

The process of simplifying is exemplified in the *Rustic capitals*, of roughly the same period as the square. They anticipate an ever-recurring tendency to condense, usually to save space. Economy was indicated when the material to write on was rare and costly vellum. For the rustic capitals, the writing instrument, held at an acute angle, causes the verticals to be thinned to the point where they become little more than a recurring beat. Against this

beat, the round and diagonal strokes make their patterns, and the horizontals provide their accent.

Much can be learned about the nature of condensed forms from these letters. If forms are essentially full or angular, they cannot be accommodated to narrow usage simply by squeezing them together. The result of such squeezing would be color-clotting in the joints of the letters.

By the fourth century, a style of writing was developed that had as its chief characteristic the rounding-off of certain angles and joints. The pen was held in a position halfway between the horizontal one, for the square, and the vertical one, for the rustic. The style of this letter was called *uncial*.

These rounded forms increased writing speed, because the curves reduced the number of strokes required of the pen. In addition, the forms flowed directly and easily from a flat-nibbed instrument. This gave them a natural authority, and legibility was enhanced. The forms most affected were A, D, E, H, M, U, and Q. Uncials continued to be written into the eighth century.

Early in the sixth century, *half uncials*, or *semiuncials* came into use. They were a true variant on capitals, and were the beginning of *minuscules*, the lowercase of type. Until that time, the alphabet had be written between two hypothetical horizontal lines. With half uncials, instead of two lines enclosing the forms, four lines were implied, as ascending and descending elements were introduced. This new variation was, again, easier to write, and had great intrinsic beauty as well. The pen was held horizontal to the line. Semiuncials belong to the seventh, eighth, and ninth centuries.

littera scripta manet

By the time that Charlemagne came to power in 768, there was considerable degeneration of calligraphic hands. No unifying force had filled the vacuum left by the dissolution of the Roman Empire, and barriers both national and natural worked against the continuity of the best forms of writing. In England and Ireland, where society was more compact and homogeneous, calligraphy fared better.

In 789 Charlemagne ordered a revision of the books of the Church. He wanted the most beautiful and accurate copies possible made of the finest existing manuscripts. The success of such an undertaking depended upon the use of a standard model that could be copied throughout the emperor's domains. The resulting model was the beautiful *Caroline minuscule*, a true small letter, with definite classic ancestry but employing the four-line

7

Littera scripta manet

system for writing. Credit for the model alphabet is given to Alcuin of York, Abbot of St. Martin's, Tours, from 796 to 804.

The style of the Caroline minuscule spread rapidly, not only throughout France and Western Europe but in England, where it was introduced in the tenth century and was generally adopted after the Norman Conquest. It is the true ancestor of the lowercase printing type in which these words are set. Its forms are simple, clear, and handsome, rounded and relatively wide.

This style tends to avoid cursive forms and excessive ligatures, especially those that would alter its inherent character. The letters are kept quite independent of each other. Curved forms that spring from straight stems have an organic relation to their source, much as a growing leaf does in nature.

In addition to looking like our lowercase, Caroline minuscules were used in much the same way. *Majuscules,* or capitals (often built up with more than a single pen stroke), began a sentence that continued in minuscules. Improvement in the organization of the written text, through better punctuation as well as sentence and paragraph arrangement, is also credited to this thoroughly constructive period. It is generally conceded that the period of the Caroline reform accomplished more than great strides in calligraphy and orthography. Without it, there would have been serious gaps in the quality of the texts which reached the Renaissance.

In spite of its wide appeal and use, this beautiful letterform in time gave way to corruptions. Divisions in style occurred, generally along geographical lines, north and south, with the writing in northern France, the Low

Countries, and England showing some kinship, and Italy, Spain, and southern France exhibiting common characteristics of style.

During the eleventh century, a general tendency toward smaller, and more condensed, letters may be noted. There was more to this compression of letters than simply change of style and economizing of space. A different rhythm began to occur, with calligraphers substituting angular, broken forms for the rounded ones. Roman capitals have a breathing rhythm; the new style, *Gothic black letter*, has the pattern of a picket fence. The regular beat of the vertical strokes and the evenness of the counters achieved an even color throughout the written page that was partly mechanical. The popularity of the *Textur* style during the mid-fifteenth century caused Gutenberg to use it as a model for his Bible type.

The diagonal couplings and footings have a pointed effect; they also serve as ter-

Littera scripta manet

minal accents, similar in function to serifs. This letter was known as *Textur* in Germany, in France as *lettre de forme*, and in England as *black letter*.

Southward, in Italy and Spain, there was strong resistance to the harsh, acute angles and fractured construction of the northern writing. A rounder Gothic, called *rotunda*, began to be written. It was as rich in color as the black letter, but it was reminiscent of the classic Roman heritage, especially as that had been expressed in the Caroline minuscule.

Littera scripta manet

Rotunda was not the only attempt to resist the angularity of the northern Gothic

littera scripta manet

style. There was also a Renaissance Roman hand known as *scrittura humanistica*, or *humanistic script*, which most directly relates our present lowercase Roman to the earlier Caroline alphabet. In the fifteenth century, enthusiasm for classic culture had been rekindled with the Renaissance, and calligraphers looked for pre-Gothic models to use in their transcriptions of classical texts. They returned to the written capitals used in the early lapidary letters, rather than merely resurrecting ninth-century writing.

The humanistic script was even more compressed than its Caroline predecessor and at the same time significantly rounder than the northern Gothics it was destined to supplant, after the introduction of printing into Italy. Early manuscripts in this script (late fourteenth and early fifteenth centuries) tended to be labored and unsteady. It was when the first great examples of printing were being produced that the humanistic script was perfected.

From the second to the fifteenth century, Roman had developed from an inscribed letter, under the influence of the chisel, through a series of pen-determined ameliorations, into a cut relief-letter that could be cast and composed for printing. The development can be shown thus:

EꟻꞒꞓee

When calligraphy reached its height, in the Renaissance, a writing hand known as *cancellaresca*, or *chancery script*, emerged. It grew out of the neo-Caroline hand, and was written with greater speed. Although there was a slant in it, slanting was not obligatory, as the cursive quality was built into the letters. The forms were more compressed than those of *scrittura humanistica*, and the rhythmic beat of nearly even strokes and space, as in black letter, created a definite pattern. Round forms became elliptical, approaching parallelograms. Roman capitals were used, but they were small in relation to the overall height of the four-line system.

Cancellaresca

About the middle of the sixteenth century, several writing manuals appeared, demonstrating the forms and flow of chancery scripts. Ludovico degli Arrighi, Giovanantonio Tagliente, and Giovanbattista Palatino are the most widely known writers of these man-uals. Their writing books are quite beautiful, yet they tend to give students a false impression of the rhythm of chancery cursive. The examples are cut in wood, and with great mastery, but they lack the spirit of the writing. Arrighi, in his introduction, "To the Kind Reader," pointed this out: "The press cannot entirely represent the living hand." This is due as much to the difficulty of putting the writing on the woodblock as to the sheer physical problems of cutting extremely small forms and at the same time maintaining color and flow.

In 1906 Edward Johnston produced the modern classic handbook for calligraphers. He tended to perpetuate the lettered characteristics of the mid-fifteenth-century manuals. Despite such physical shortcomings in presentation, chancery has shown itself more capable of becoming a universally recognized hand (for Westerners) than any other.

II ANATOMY

BOARDMAN ROBINSON, the distinguished American draftsman, advised his students to observe and depict the spine of a model as the stabilizing factor in the figure's actions. Henri Matisse suggested that an artist assume the model's pose: where the strain comes is the key to the movement. Skeletal concepts have several virtues when applied to the anatomy of the alphabet. For one thing, the value of accepting letters as having characteristics of living organisms is indicated. One of the hazards faced by the calligrapher is his urge to improve on a repeated letter, to embellish it. But whereas, for example, in music Mozart could improvise endlessly, it was his discipline that made him choose among improvisations and continue the development of a theme.

Although efforts to formulate the letter symbols must end in individual apperceptions, it is valuable to restate what is most universal in the skeletal anatomy of the Roman alphabet. An understanding of the twenty-six letters as simple geometric archetypes is the key to providing the imagination with a set of armatures on which to model the forms, as individually as a sculptor might model a figure in clay. The illustration of sculptor-in-clay should be expanded to include sculptor-in-stone and typecutter-in-steel, for the armature need not be material. It can exist very powerfully as an imaginary skeletal structure. Here, Robinson's comment on the spine as key to action and stability is applicable to letters, for the form must be balanced within itself. There are optical forces that are as relentless as gravity. Goethe said that the human form cannot be comprehended merely by seeing its surface.

13

He thought it must be stripped of muscles and the joints observed for action and counteraction, if we would "see and imitate what moves as a beautiful, inseparable whole in living waves before the eye." And Heinrich Woelfflin found that "beauty is clarity of articulation."

The 1920s witnessed numerous efforts aimed at simplifying letter forms and restating them in relation to function. Like any self-conscious aesthetic, this one was only partly successful. The new style in letters was most generally realized in sans serif forms, strictly rationalized and constructed. One of the best typefaces to come out of that period was Paul Renner's *Futura*, still in use after half a century. Another was *Kabel*, a formalization of the single-stroke Roman capitals that Rudolph Koch used as beginning exercises in his calligraphy classes at Offenbach's Technische Lehranstalt. Koch's concept was nearer the classic model than Renner's.

A small writing-book that was published in 1930, *Das Schreibbüchlein*, and the foundry showing of *Kabel* reproduced a set of diagrams drawn by Koch and cut in wood by Fritz Kredel. In seven woodcuts, the twenty-six Roman capitals are divided into groups and set against squares. The value of using square fields to visualize the proportion and articulation of the basic skeletal symbols has been mentioned earlier. These Koch-Kredel diagrams have the advantage of great simplicity, of both conception and realization. They are used here, in conjunction with *Kabel* capitals.

The first figure combines four letters: A, I, T, and V, all of which are symmetrical. The triangular forms, A and V, fill the square. T is an implied triangular form, which because of its open sides requires a horizontal that is less than the full width for optical reasons, and to achieve a more graceful relationship between the horizontal and vertical elements. I, with T, falls into the symmetrical grouping, because it too has a full-height vertical.

Anyone who wants to design letters starts with the skeletal forms, then combines them into words, phrases, and sentences. A pen capable of producing an even-weight line and inexpensive cross-section paper are the first needed supplies. At the outset, it is instructive to put the lines of lettering close together, because this shows up the color of the work and calls attention to areas of poor letterspacing or improper handling of joints that can cause clotting.

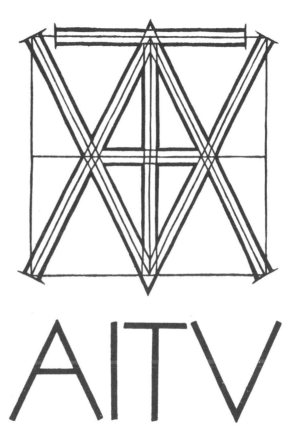

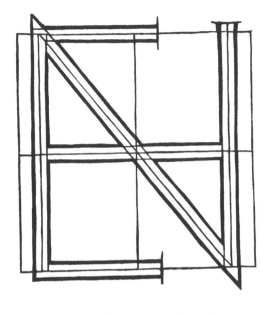

Figure 2 shows E. F. L, N, and H. The first three are narrow forms that are based on half of a square. Their relationship to each other is obvious as three possible variations of a vertical with one, two, and three half-width horizontals. The group as a whole is dominated by vertical elements. N and H have the same width, and each has verticals with connecting members, one horizontal, the other diagonal. It is important that these connectors unify the stems, rather than drive them apart.

EFLNH

X, Y, and Z are presented in figure 3. The width of this group is narrower than H and N and is comparable to T in the first diagram. Another similarity to figure 1 is the symmetrical aspect of X and Y.

Spacing between letters is kept even by an awareness of the *areas* of each letter shape. For example, the space between vertical letters is very easy to judge. On the other hand, in the case of fall-away letters such as A and O, it is necessary to imagine a vertical passing through them, equalizing the plus and minus of their configuration. Modern usage has tended to crowd letters together, sometimes for a certain effect but more often to save space. The classic feeling of more open spacing is still to be preferred. In the shapes of letters, there are a number of inherent problems of spacing that can only be solved by accepting their existence and achieving optical evenness by accommodation.

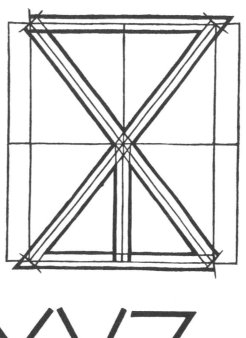

17

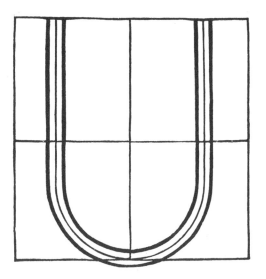

U and J (figure 4) have been identified as late arrivals in the developing Roman alphabet: U as an outgrowth of the V form and J as an alternate of I. It is worth noting that U, in principle, is an inverted Roman arch, a shape that is functionally strong in the architectural position. As a letter symbol, the half round becomes a rocker. This aspect is sometimes helped by extending the right stem, to make it a full-length vertical, thus improving variety as well as stability.

Figure 5 brings together the exclusively round forms: G, O, Q, and S, with O as a full circle, filling the square. It is important to think of it in this way, for the integrity of a symbol lies to a great extent in the simplicity of its conception as an archetype. Neither an archetype nor a model is to be merely copied. In lettering as in drawing, distortion is only the graphic means of presenting a more fully realized form. "The artist's object," said Delacroix, "is not to reproduce exactly, for he would at once be stopped by the impossibility of doing so. It is the *spirit* of the subject that he tries to realize." In this group, S is thought of as two semicircles set together to produce a continuous flow that reverses on itself. As in B, any differentiation in the upper and lower sections is chiefly for optical reasons.

C is indicated by a white stroke in G.

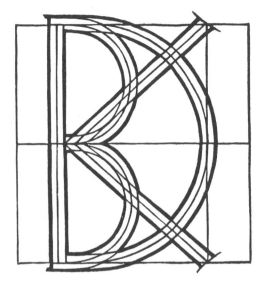

BDKPR

Grouped in figure 6 are the four letters that combine verticals and half rounds: B, D, P, and R, plus K, related to R by sharing a vertical stem and short diagonal tail. Although in theory the symbol composed of a vertical and a semicircle is satisfactory, in practice a short flat passage before the curve begins will help provide the round element with its proper fullness.

The letters shown in the seven figures in this section are presented in simplest geometric terms. From time to time it has been noted that the eye must make adjustments to improve the inner stability of the parts of a letter and the relationships of these parts to each other. This means increasing the height of elements that tend to fall away from the top or bottom lines and adjusting the division of letters with upper and lower halves. In B and E, the two lower sections can be increased. In A, the crossbar needs to be lowered.

Finally, M and W, the two forms that are wider than high, are shown in figure 7. Both letters, because of their angular joints, are particularly sensitive to condensation.

The perfect expression of a skeletal alphabet, of archetypes, is the one that comes closest to realizing symbol and image as one. In his advice to letter artists, John Howard Benson counseled, "You will never see good letters coming from your hand until you have learned to see good letters in your head." Edgar Degas had much the same thought in mind when he proposed a five-storied art school, where the beginners would start, drawing from the model on the top floor, and as they improved would be promoted downward, where checking on the model would require more and more effort.

21

III ROMAN CAPITALS

ONLY BY UNDERSTANDING the internal mechanism can the outside be fully delineated. Thus Emerson explained Michelangelo's dedication to anatomical mastery. The skeletons of letters are no less important in determining and rendering their fleshed-out forms. By accepting Roman capitals as archetypical symbols, deviations from them can be classified as what they really are: a kind of shorthand, or stand-ins *(in locum tenens)* for the originals. It has been noted that despite numerous digressions from the basically geometric, the alphabet has managed to remain essentially Roman because of repeated efforts to reestablish the classic concept. In the fifteenth century, black letter received added impetus because Gutenberg and his immediate followers chose it for their types. But the calligraphers of the time were also employing, with the pen, the essential shapes and rhythms that had been carved in stone thirteen centuries before in Rome. Therefore, it seems fitting to choose for showing here a handling of weights and stresses similar to those of the humanistic majuscules of the Renaissance.

A writing instrument fashioned with a flat edge will stress lines according to the way it is held and handled. To produce a calligraphic Roman, in which the relationships of heavy and light strokes of verticals and horizontals are comparable to those found in the Trajan inscription, it is necessary to hold the pen at slanted stress in the round and half-round elements. The secret of stability in such strokes lies in imagining the skeleton at the center of the swelling weight.

The top line of letters here illustrates the simple use of a flat pen. Those below are the

23

ABC

ABC

24

same characters with serifs added by a flat pen of narrow width. The slight bracketing relates these written serifs to their carved ancestors.

A as written here has been narrowed from its full symbol triangulation, as a means of moderating the fall-away effect and thus easing spacing. The crossbar is somewhat lowered from the median and lightened to open and improve the relationship of the upper and lower counters.

B when made with a pen held at a slant can easily show a slight enlargement of the lower bowl. The value of this optical correction has been observed earlier in discussing the skeletal symbols.

C is the first of the full-round forms. In it, and in D and O, the curves should have a continuing flow. The open aspect of the big, round letters contributes greatly to the essential rhythm of Roman capitals. These letters also demand adequate letterspacing through-out a word.

D might be compared to C in most essentials. The vertical, as it joins with the curve, demands a short flat passage, to give the resulting bowl the appearance of a complete half round, and again to improve stability.

E and Z are the only letters touching both the top and bottom lines with horizontal elements. Some correction in height may be called for when these letters come between angular or tangential shapes that give them the appearance of being too tall.

F has many of the characteristics of E, as it functions in the rhythm of the line. Its full-length stem and narrow half-width horizontals are complete variations on the O.

DEF

DEF

GHI

GHI

G is related to C in width. Its stem, however, gives it very special qualities in composition. Because this added element, the stem, affects the counter of the letter, G has less tendency to cut a hole in a written or printed word.

H poses the problem of connecting two strong verticals rather than driving them apart. In general, the height of the letter is greater than its width. H is a good example of this rule of thumb at work.

I is at once the simplest and the narrowest of all the letters. As the alphabet is studied, it becomes increasingly apparent that expansion and contraction in the Roman line, from narrow I to wide O, are essentials of its character.

J is a variant of I. If its tail is kept to a mere telling gesture of the pen, that is sufficient to establish its identity. As a beginning letter, however, or in highly decorative inscriptions, the tail can be elaborated.

K is sometimes made with a flowing tail, but it reflects its geometric nature best when it is composed of a full vertical touched at its center by a right angle. For example, the stonecutters advise a minimal junction with the stem.

L has a built-in spacing problem. It is an asymmetrical letter exposing an open counter, which is greatly aggravated when it falls next to an A. Adjustments in its relation to C, G, O, Q, T, V, W, and Y are much more easily made.

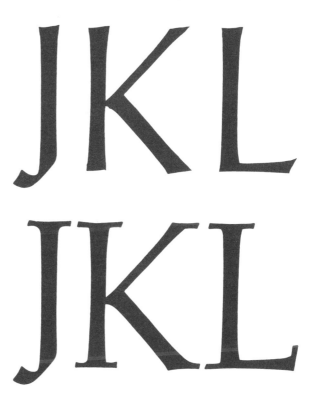

27

M is a wide letter, described in the second section as being greater in width than height. Here, the classic formula is compromised sufficiently to resist a possible sprawl in the letter. However, the character of M, including the spread of strokes, has been kept.

N like H, calls for a relationship among its three elements that will make it optically stable. The verticals should appear to be unified by the diagonal, rather than merely joined. The slanted pen gives classic stress to the diagonal.

28

O has great importance in setting the whole style of an alphabet, in form, appearance, and character. The thrust of the pen strokes must resist roll and back slope, by keeping the skeleton within the swelling curves.

P having the simplest of the small curved forms, calls for some increase in the size of its bowl to compensate for the open space below. In the carry-through of the lower juncture with the vertical, this compensation can be made quite naturally.

QR
QR

Q is an O with a tail, and the most important aspect of this adjunct is that it identifies Q. As in the case of J, a small gesture of the pen may be sufficient. Q is, of course, always followed by U.

R has an element in its lower half below the bowl. As in K, this diagonal should give the appearance of springing from the stem of the letter. It should also be joined to the stem so that the crotch of the lower counter remains as open as possible.

S is the setting together of two halves of a circle in such a way that one half moves continuously into the other. To achieve stability and correct any back-sloping tendency, the joined elements are rotated clockwise.

T when made with a slanted pen has the horizontal-vertical weight relationship associated with the great Trajan inscription. The length of the horizontal is most important to the affinity of the two elements, and to establishing the counterspaces of the letter.

U is one of the added letters. It should be noted, again, that a circular joining of the letter's two verticals can be strengthened and made easier to produce with a pen if the right-hand stroke is made as a full vertical.

STU

STU

V like O, is a genetic form. It is the basis for forming M and W and has most of the characteristics of A. In each of these letters, care must be taken to keep the inner angles open, to avoid clotting. All pointed elements must be kept strong at point of contact to the line, in order to maintain even height.

W was introduced into England by French scribes in the eleventh century. It is a ligatured letter, made by overlapping VV or UU. To avoid darkening, the overlap can be implied, as it is here. W, originally a ligature, is now considered a single letter symbol.

X although made up of crossed elements is not a cross. The angled joints of X are critical to the appearance of the letter, and the upper and lower counters must remain open so that the crossing does not darken.

Y should be somewhat similar to X in the size and angle of its upper half. Both echo the V form at half height, and both are better when they resist sprawl. With the V part of the shape on the narrow side, the flow of the stem from the joint is more elegant.

Z again, is a letter with top and bottom horizontals, and these can give it the appearance of unusual height. As in the case of E, optical correction is necessary. The diagonal line, from upper right to lower left, becomes thin when produced with a slanted flat pen.

XYZ

XYZ

IV ROMAN SMALL LETTERS

BACKGROUND MATERIAL in the first section of this book is a kind of chronicle of the efforts, lasting more than a millennium, to achieve practical written substitutes for the classic carved Roman alphabet. Two basic directions were noted in those more than a thousand years of calligraphy: one leading eventually to heavy, angular forms and the other to rounder and more open ones. The former was doomed centuries ago when the great Roman printing types of Jenson, Aldus, and Garamond appeared, even though several varieties of black letter continued in use in Germany well into the 1930s. The Roman branch of the tree flourished, and modifications that were made between the second and sixteenth centuries can be reduced to three main categories: rounding of forms, introduction of ascending and descending elements,

and finally a reimposition of the classic spirit on the evolved minuscules.

There is good reason to choose the humanistic minuscule (*scrittura humanistica*) as the model for examples of what is generally called *Roman small letter*, or *lowercase*. It is a product of the flowering of calligraphy and represents a period, the Renaissance, when calligraphers as well as painters and architects had cast off the anonymity of the Middle Ages. Outstanding writers and manuals on writing were numerous, and good calligraphy was almost as commonplace as folk art. It was the time of Raphael, who wrote as beautifully as anyone who ever lived. Later, in succeeding centuries, letterforms were increasingly influenced by printing. In its turn, printing responded to the stylistic pull of engraving. Handwriting was also inspired by the burin, and writing masters

35

abcdefgh

forsook literary forms for more clerkly ones.

The most basic changes from uncials, half-uncials, and Caroline to humanistic minuscules show themselves in straightened vertical stems and the addition of serifs. Both are characteristic of the Roman spirit.

A look at the Section I examples of uncials and Caroline minuscules indicates the intermediate stages of **a** as leg and crossbar are joined, rounded, and reduced. The letter **b** is one of several instances where part of a letter has been allowed to atrophy, in favor of its identifying characteristic, here, the lower

bowl. The letter **c** has remained unchanged, but **d** is greatly altered, its straight and curved elements having shifted left and right. A glance back to Section I will also show several stages in the changing of the letter **e**, from the rounding of the vertical and top and bottom horizontals to the coupling of the upper stroke and crossbar. The letter **f** has become narrow and is an ascending letter. The letter **g**, like **a**, is less recognizable as the offspring of its clas-

Dᴏᴆd

ijklmnop

g533

sic ancestor. This is essentially a case of the tail wagging the dog. The terminal stem of the Roman capital developed a descending tail in its uncial form. Closing the normal opening on the right had begun before the eighth century.

The letter **h**, in early cursive writing, had lost the upper half of its right-hand vertical stem, and the crossbar became rounded.

The dot over the letter **i** is a modification of a sign, like an acute accent, that was used to distinguish it from adjoining letters with similar stems. It was in the seventeenth century that **i** and **j** were consistently differentiated as vowel and consonant. The letter **k** and **l** are both characteristic of the early minuscules, in the exaggeration of stems that came with the four-line system of the half uncials. The right angle of **l** became a rounded vestigial tail in the Caroline hand and finally gave way to the present simple vertical. In the fourth century, rounds had been substituted for the angles in **m**. The uncials of that period retained the essentials of **n**, and the practice was generally

37

qrstuvw

continued in the half uncials. The present shape of **n** was developed in the insular half uncials and the Caroline minuscules. Examples in Section I show this, as well as the straightening of the first stroke of **m**. The letter **o** retains its full identification with O. The examples cited for **m** and **n** serve to illustrate the introduction of a descending stem for the half uncial **p**, and its perpetuation in the Caroline hand.

The descending tail of **q** shows again the influence of the stress aspect of early Roman cursive on the half uncial form. The letter **r** as a Roman small letter became a shorthand symbol of its classic ancestor.

The letter **s** retains its original form. The long **s** (see half uncial illustration in Section I) is no longer used in English. The minuscule **t** is a simplification of the rounded uncial.

Both **u** and **v** are completely recognizable small letter versions of their Roman originals, as is the minuscule **w**. The last retains the joined **v** forms, rather than employing the double **u** which could be more open and less sensitive in joints. However, the use of such simple geometric shapes helps retain some of

XYZ

the flavor of the Roman prototype.

Finally, x, y, and z are little changed by their excursion through the Middle Ages. The letter y has become a descending letter, but its essential tailed-v form remains. Y comes from the Greek upsilon, via the Latin. It is from the same source as U, V, and W (Semitic), and this kinship has been maintained in the structural resemblances.

The most important single observation to be made about Roman small letters is to see them as stand-ins, or surrogates, for the capitals. They represent a continuing search for a working alphabet, a search that has been going on for the better part of the past eighteen hundred years. That fact in itself gives them status and authority.

These are reduced forms, and as a result the counters are also reduced. This, in turn, means that letterspacing need not be as generous as in the case of the capitals. While capitals have an air of majesty and lend themselves to display, small letters are meant for the words, the line, and the mass. In composition, they have a texture that is as important to the look of a page of text as are the smaller rhythms within words. Ascending and descending elements of small letters have certain practical virtues, as well as being decorative. They not only demand and assure line-spacing, they also provide an added identification of their own, a kind of handle by which the eye can quickly get hold of the symbol. Thus, they serve their primary purpose—legibility.

39

V THE LIVING ALPHABET

ALKING THE STREETS OF ROME in the second half of the twentieth century, one is constantly reminded of the grandeur that once was; one views his surroundings as monuments to the past. But there are those past monuments, arches and columns, that bear inscriptions in an alphabet as alive today as it was in the time of Caesar. The word *vitality* comes to mind for such long life. Vitality's synonyms are life, animation, vital power, vigor, virility—all of which can be used to describe the Roman capitals.

It is little short of a miracle that a set of symbols is able to last so long, unless these symbols have inherent qualities akin to the regenerative processes found in living organisms. The periodic reincarnation of the classic Roman forms, from the time of Trajan to our own, may even evidence some of the meta-

physical properties of immortality. Part of this long, and recurring, life may be due to the relatively pure aspect of this set of abstract symbols, with all the virtues of their formal geometric framework. It is not too difficult to describe the Roman alphabet in words alone, something that would be impossible to conceive in the case of Chinese or Arabic characters.

Pythagoras described music as a "hieroglyphical and shadowed lesson of the whole world," and Aristotle reinforced the thought with this observation that "there seems to be a sort of relationship between the soul on the one hand and harmonies and rhythm on the other." Music and poetry, painting and sculpture are all music, in its Greek and widest sense, according to Macneile Dixon, in his *Human Situation*. He names as the rhythmical sisterhood the ordered and shapely, the measured, the flowing, and the melodious. "Rhythm appears to be the distinctive and peculiar dialect or style of the soul—its idiom or vernacular," says Dixon.

Certainly the *soul* or *spirit* of the alphabet is in its rhythm, and there must be very few who have been deeply involved with letters who have failed to sense it. This is not so much a matter of theory as of feeling, just as Titian's realization of the role of color in painting must have arisen from sensibility rather than cerebration, supreme craftsman though he was. No greater demonstration of insensitivity to the breathing rhythm of Roman capitals exists than the frequent attempts to crowd letters together without sufficient space. *The forms demand air to breathe.*

In the past, the chief degenerative forces that pressed relentlessly on calligraphy were, besides poor communication and the inbred nature of the calligraphic community, a lack of a sophisticated and demanding audience. Often, writers did not know what they were writing and were merely copying shapes instead of words or thoughts. And it may be true that "the ear and the eye doth make us deaf and blind."

Such a period of degeneration in writing, at the beginning of the reign of Charlemagne, led to the significant accomplishments of his reforms. The emperor was able to put the results of his efforts into the widest possible circulation. But the high standards of the Caroline minuscule could not be indefinitely maintained. Its influence became fragmented, largely along lines of differing national, political, or geographical boundaries.

An emerging secular literature began to exert pressure on the shape of letters. In the fourteenth century, writing began to bear the mark of definite personalities: Chaucer in England and Boccaccio, Dante, and Petrarch in Italy are examples. The Middle English in which Chaucer wrote became the basis for standardization of our language.

An influence on letters, more profound than any other during the intervening years since Roman times, was the arrival of the printing press in the latter half of the fifteenth century. The press provided a means of making letter styles transportable and minimized the effect of geography on the acceptance of common forms. The political turmoil that sent a number of printers from Germany into Italy, first to Subiaco and finally to Venice, hastened the ascendancy of Roman as a model for Western alphabets.

Progress, unfortunately, is not a steadily advancing procession, as the word tends to imply. It is better, perhaps, to associate progress with Sisyphus than with a relentless Father Time. Printing, with its accompanying proliferation and mechanization, brought new threats to a continuing and simple Roman letter, as routine was substituted for direct human involvement. And there was a gradual disappearance of the great body of calligraphers who had conscientiously kept the alphabet alive, contributing to its maintenance and the survival of learning itself.

What might be described as a temporary eclipse for the Roman alphabets of Jenson and Garamond was at the same time a period of great gains for literature. The medium of printing continued, in the nineteenth century for example, to bring the art of literary composition to great heights, and simultaneously enlarged the reading audience.

The letterforms and fat type styles of the first half of the nineteenth century were viewed with dismay by an English publisher named William Pickering. With Charles Whittingham of the Chiswick Press, Pickering revived William Caslon's *Old Face* (old style) type of the century before and put it to use with some of the typographic style of an even earlier period. The influence of the early Roman inscriptions is reflected in the bracketed serifs of an old style.

The waning authority of classic models was bolstered by another, seemingly insignificant, force. The Kelmscott Press, set up by William Morris in 1891, was a small operation by any standards. The recharged atmosphere brought about by the handful of co-workers is more important than are the works of Morris themselves. Within a decade after the founding of the Kelmscott Press, the alphabet was being reexamined as it had not been for decades, even centuries. In 1906 Edward Johnston's *Writing and Illuminating* was published. It begins thus: "Nearly every type of letter with which we are familiar is derived from Roman Capitals, and has come to us through the me-

dium, or been modified by the influence, of the pen." Through his book and his teaching, Johnston managed a small renaissance on his own that is still felt in the best calligraphers, type makers, and to some degree architects and stonecutters. Though no claim can be made for a calligraphic ambience such as that of the early sixteenth century, the twentieth, in its first four decades, witnessed a growth in discrimination and an increase in the number of artists who became interested in the design of type and illustration. Thus some antidote was provided for the dehumanizing pressures of mechanization.

In the past, technical innovations have usually affected the appearance of letterforms through the uninformed, or insensitive, efforts of an inventor desiring to make them fit the limitations of his creation. An example would be the common typewriter, which assigns the same space to all the characters, wide and narrow, large and small. A by-product of the same machine's use is the withering away of manual writing talents, as the mechanical system is substituted. It is reasonable to assume that in the second half of the twentieth century the average person growing up will have little basis for judging what is good or bad in the letters he sees about him. Certainly he can not be expected to have an instinctive feeling about their forms.

The electronic assault on alphabet archetypes is different from the merely mechanical or technical ones of the past. Some letterforms must now be able to be read by a robot; others must be produced by impulses coming at incredible speeds. Neither of these demands made on the letter is related to aesthetics or to any cultural experience. At a time when reading proficiency is found to be scandalously declining, society is faced with the prospect of more and more devices capable of relieving almost everyone of the drudgery of thought. Yet Pascal said, "All our dignity consists in thought," and there can be little doubt that it is the most uniquely human of accomplishments.

Delacroix, in his *Journal*, wrote in a most illuminating way about the use of a model. Essentially, a model enables the artist to simplify forms that his imagination tends to elaborate, for fear of omitting a salient feature. This describes quite accurately the experience of the best of those who have produced letterforms over the past centuries. The ones least sure of the bare symbol have been the most profligate with dressmaker details. When the Roman alphabet was given its first great translation into type—roughly in the last years of the fifteenth century and the beginning of the sixteenth—the means used were sculptural. The type designer worked from a concept rather than a drawing, and his purpose was to

LITTERA SCRIPTA MANET

reveal the form of a letter rather than to build it up. Letters were cut in the sizes in which they were conceived. Nearly five hundred years later, attitudes about scale have changed completely. The camera gives the impression that letters can be enlarged or reduced at will, all sizes coming from a single master pattern. There has been no change in the sensitivity of the human eye to proportion: it is the experience back of the eye that has become desensitized.

The concept of a Living Alphabet is not strained. The descriptive phrase is justified when one thinks of the extraordinary longevity of the Roman capitals and of their rebirth in variations over the centuries. But the capacity to be reborn does not always carry with it the necessary sustenance to life and growth, as witness every endangered species. A powerful awareness of endangerment is necessary, to rally meaningful forces to work for survival.

Time may provide a counteraction to the headlong improvisations demanded by electronic duplication. Until such a time comes, there is no way for the collective vision to be protected from the debased product that may have become acceptable through extensive use. Bad letterforms, like bad money, may be assumed to drive out good.

The Living Alphabet is best understood if the purely physical features of letterforms can somehow be penetrated and the indestructible elements recognized and held as the quintessence of abstraction. To be looked for is the imperishable core. This has been identified here as the soul, or the spirit, of the symbol. Its simplest physical expression, in structure and articulation, is geometric, and its rhythm is a breathing one of expanding and contracting configurations. The skeleton of a Roman capital is a remarkably describable archetype, having proved itself capable of crossing barriers of language and space.

There ought to be no question as to the value of maintaining the Roman alphabet in its noblest form as the Western master pattern for written and printed communication. If electronic scanning devices cannot read it, then their acceptable symbols must be regarded as merely sign language, or a makeshift shorthand. They should not be allowed to impinge on the aesthetic and humanizing values that have been derived from the classical letter forms. Arrighi said, "The press cannot entirely represent the living hand," and his observation might be applied to any purely mechanical solution.

Along with a commitment to the perpetuation of the archetypes should go constant pressure to maintain as high standards as possible for the learning and practice of writing and reading. Instead of these accomplishments having the air of drudgery about them, they ought better to be thought of as achievements and as communication. For students, it would be helpful and instructive to come upon the inexpensive little *Book of Scripts* by Alfred Fairbank. They could learn from it how to write a good hand. Enough such students would guarantee the survival and vigor of the Living Alphabet, and keep language alive as well.

Afterword

IN 1935, shortly after a year of work with Rudolf Koch in his Offenbacher Werkstatt, I wrote *The of Anatomy Lettering*. It was undertaken primarily as a memorial to Koch, after his death in 1934. My hope was to present letters as a concept rather than an expression of style. Forty years later, I am no less impressed by the function of the bones and joints of letters in determining the fundamental character of the alphabet.

In 1970 *A Short History of the Printed Word* was published. In it, I attempted to respond to a request that I tell the story of type, its background and use. An integral part of that story is, of course, the alphabet and its development over some twelve hundred years, from Trajan's Rome to Gutenberg's Mainz. At that time, it seemed to me that the material which had been brought together in the short history should

be expanded into a discussion of some of the philosophical and aesthetic properties of the alphabet and given a presentation of its own. I am grateful to the director and board of the University Press of Virginia for providing this opportunity to bring that idea into being.

My grandfather John Chappell did some lettering and decorative design from the 1870s until his death in 1915. And my cousin Oscar

Ogg may have been partly influenced by the interests of that mutual ancestor in deciding to put aside his plans for an architectural career and follow me into the graphic arts. At the Art Students League, I was closely associated with Allen Lewis, who was also the teacher of John Howard Benson. At that time, in the 1920s, Frederic W. Goudy conducted an annual series of lectures at the League. At the beginning of the 1930s, in the Werkstatt, I came to have the friendship of Fritz Kredel and Berthold Wolpe. In time, through Berthold, I met Alfred Fairbank, whose friendship I greatly value today. To all these, friends and co-workers in the graphic arts, and to the protagonist, the Roman alphabet, I dedicate this book.

THIS BOOK

is set in Trajanus, designed for D. Stempel AG, Frankfurt am Main, by Warren Chappell. The composition has been done by the Finn Typographic Service of Stamford, Connecticut. The printing and binding are by Kingsport Press, Inc. of Kingsport, Tennessee. The typographic design is by the author, as are the illustrations, with the exception of those identified as being by Rudolf Koch.